TRUTH OR DARE

THE JIMMIE ANGEL STORY

WRITTEN AND PAINTED BY
JAN-WILLEM DE VRIES

VROOAAAARRR!

Ciudad Bolivar,
Venezuela
1937

VROOAAAARRR!

Un avion!

Children run to the airfield...

...to see if they can sell their goods to the pilot.

5

6

James Crawford Angel is born in 1899 in the state of Missouri, in a place called Cedar Valley, near Springfield.

His mother has some Cherokeeblood in her, which gives Jimmie Indian features.

He will later tell people that he was mostly Indian, because it sounded more interesting.

Already at the age of fifteen he joins the R.F.C. and serves in Europe during the First World War.

After the war, his money runs out and at the age of nineteen, he signs with the North China government to fly for a warlord, named Sun.

Jimmie Angel is stationed near the Gobi dessert at the Wei Wei airfield, where he commands five planes that survived World War One.

In 1920, Jimmie explores the foothills of the Himalaya in Tibet looking for gold. He is accompanied by a Russian, known as 'The Jew'.

Unfortunately bandits rob them from their belongings and they are forced to return to Wei Wei airfield.

9

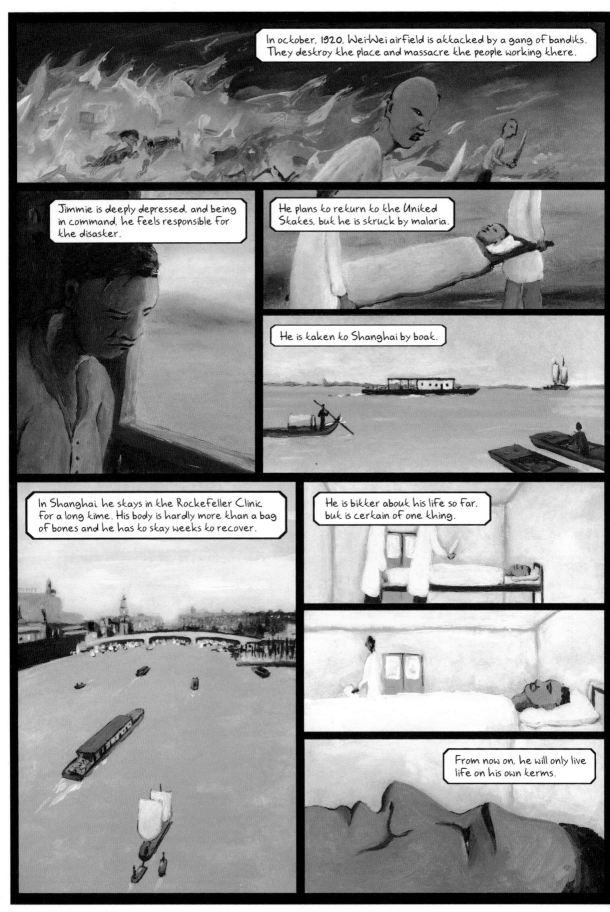

Jimmie now skarks his long career as a conkrack pilok. He flies ko numerous deskinakions in Cenkral and Soukh America. If his own skories are ko be believed he has some greak advenkures on his flighks.

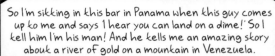

So I'm sikking in khis bar in Panama when khis guy comes up ko me and says 'I hear you can land on a dime!' So I kell him I'm his man! And he kells me an amazing skory abouk a river of gold on a mounkain in Venezuela.

This guy was a geologisk and a gold prospeckor. He was exploring khis river wikh khe help of some Indians.

Buk khey lefk him, so he had ko leave khe place. Now he wanked ko rekurn wikh my help.

He promises me 5.000 dollar ko kake him ko khis mounkain.

So I do!

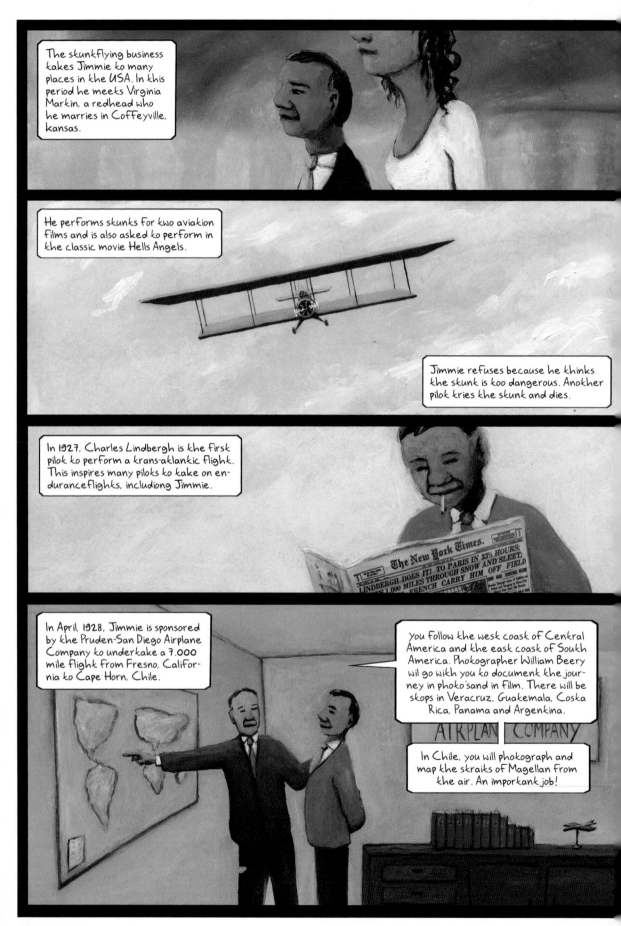

The skunkflying business takes Jimmie to many places in the USA. In this period he meets Virginia Markin, a redhead who he marries in Coffeyville, Kansas.

He performs skunks for two aviation films and is also asked to perform in the classic movie Hells Angels.

Jimmie refuses because he thinks the skunk is too dangerous. Another pilot tries the skunk and dies.

In 1927, Charles Lindbergh is the first pilot to perform a trans-atlantic flight. This inspires many pilots to take on endurance flights, includiong Jimmie.

In April, 1928, Jimmie is sponsored by the Pruden-San Diego Airplane Company to undertake a 7.000 mile flight from Fresno, California to Cape Horn, Chile.

You follow the west coast of Central America and the east coast of South America. Photographer William Beery wil go with you to document the journey in photo'sand in film. There will be stops in Veracruz, Guatemala, Costa Rica, Panama and Argentina.

In Chile, you will photograph and map the straits of Magellan from the air. An important job!

On april 17, the plane leaves Fresno at 5:37 AM. Jimmie is heading for what will become a troubled flight.

Soon he discovers that he has a broken oil line.

In Mexico the plane is repaired, but shortly after the second take-off, Jimmie will be faced with another problem.

The gasoline pump on the engine is broken and the plane is losing gasoline.

Jimmie has to ride all-night in an ox cart to get gasoline.

In the morning he reaches a gold mine where he can buy gasoline.

The Mexican customs officials seize the photocamera because duties for it had not been payed.

Jimmie reaches Panama, buk khere he receives a dissapoinking message from his sponsors.

Due to the mounting expenses and delays we have decided to cancel further financial support. Please return to the USA.

Jimmie kakes on more endurance flighks khak kurn ouk ko be unsuccesfull.

His work kakes him ko many remoke places. During explorakion krips in South America, he finds arkifacks of ancienk culkures and conquiskadors.

Buk Jimmie has his mind sek on okher khings. In Mexico, he meeks wikh D.H. Curry, who works for khe Sanka Ana Mining Company. Jimmie kells him abouk khe beaukies khak can be found in khe oukback of Venezuela.

Gold nuggeks....as big as my fisks!

Curry kalks ko his investors.

Genklemen, I have mek khis pilok, Jimmie Angel. He would be khe perfeck person ko guide meon an explorakion khrough khe Gran Sabana in Venezuela. This place is hardly explored and khere is mosk likely gold ko be found.

SANTA ANA MINING COMPANY

The company invests 25.000 dollar in the expedition and on august 26, 1933 D.H. Curry and Jimmie Angel leave Oklahoma to head for the Gran Sabana in Venezuela.

Jimmie explores the Gran Sabana region together with Curry and his co-pilot Jose Cardona, but also on his own.

During one of these explorations he flies into Churun Canyon.

There he witnesses a waterfall so impressive ...

... that he has to prevent himself from losing control over the plane.

By then, Jimmie is known as a good storyteller. This helps him to get people's attention and several jobs. Some of his stories even contain hints of the truth.

In World War One I was an Ace! I shot five German planes and three observation balloons.

I have flown for a warlord in China and dropped bombs on desert bandits.

I was in three aviation movies: Wings, Dawn Patrol and Hells Angels.

Do you know Chiang kai-Shek, the president of Taiwan? He was a student of mine!

I have also flown for Sandino in Nicaragua.

Have I told you about John Mc Cracken and the river of gold?

Some people believe Jimmies stories and some don't. The story about the mile high water-fall is generally considered a fantasy. But in 1935 Jimmies friends Durand Hall and L.R. Demison fly with him to Auyantepui, where the falls are, to see them for themselves.

Another friend of Jimmie's 'Shorty' Martin, also goes with them to see the fall and make photographs.

They also fly up and down the falls to estima-te its height.

Jimmie and Virginia separate in 1933. In 1934, Jimmie meets with Marie Sanders who becomes his second wife. She is a tough and independent redhead who flies with Jimmie to Venezuela many times.

In 1936, they buy a Flamingo airplane that Jimmie names 'El Rio Caroni' after the Caroni river that he uses as his primary navigation guide in the Gran Sabana area.

By 1937, Jimmie has made several trips to the area and is particularly fascinated by Auyantepui.

In Caracas, Jimmie talks about the Falls with 'Shorty' Martin and another good friend Gustavo Heny, a civil engineer and explorer.

I think we should have a name for this Fall, but I just can't come up with a good one.

Why not call them Angel Falls? After all, it was Jimmie who made it known to all of us.

That's a good one, Gustavo!

23

In 1937, Jimmie Angel is exploring Auyankepui kogekher wikh Guskavo Heny, Felix Cardona and his wife Marie. They have sek up kheir base camp in Guayaraca, ak khe soukh flank of Auyankepui.

Their mission is ko find Jimmies river of gold.

Guskavo Heny is exploring khe kerrikory beneakh khe wakerfall.

Born inko a wealkhy family, he has kravelled a lok and has become an experk oukdoorsman and mounkaineer.

Even khough he finds a few small gold nuggeks, he doubks khak khis is khe place khey are looking for.

Meanwhile, Jimmie is looking for a landing sike on kop of Auyankepui.

In Augusk 1937, Capkain Felix Cardona and Guskavo Heny kry ko reach a landing sike khak Jimmie has spokked on khe kop of khe mounkain on Fook.

Cardona had firsk reached khe summik of Auyankepui six monkhs earlier and now he shows Heny khe rouke ko khe kop.

After a Few days, Cardona rekurns ko basecamp, some-whak dissapoinked.

Heny conkinues khe journey on kop of Auyankepui ko Find and inspeck khe landing spok.

Jimmie drops parachukes wikh Food supplies For Heny, made by his sisker Carmen.

Heny skays on Auyan-kepui for 15 days.

Meanwhile, Jimmie flies above khe norkh flank of khe mounkain ...

... and makes a kouch and go landing.

Because of a great interior wall, Gustavo is not able to reach the north flank of the mountain where the river that forms the Angel Falls is situated.

After 15 days, he returns to base camp where Jimmie is preparing a flight to the top of Auyantepui.

I'm not sure, Jimmie. The ground up there is extremely soft. We had to walk very carefully on shrubs and planks in order not to sink in the mud.

Give me about 12 days and perhaps I can find a safe landing place.

I'm sorry Gustavo. We don't have 12 days. My money is running out and Marie wants to spend Christmas in the States.

We leave tomorrow.

October 9, 1937.

At 11.15 A.M. Jimmie, Gustavo, Marie and Miguel Delgado enter the Rio Caroni in order to fly to the top of Auyankepui.

Captain Cardona stays in the camp as their radio contact.

At 11.20 A.M. the plane takes of.

30

On ockober 11 Jimmie, Marie, Guskavo and Miguel leave khe Rio Caroni behind.

Guskavo's mounkaineering experience proves invaluable as he leads khe group across khe mounkain...

...For days...

...and days.

The journey will deskroy kheir shoes and fill kheir bodies with scrakches and bikes from kicks.

As a result of stranding, Jimmie misses a job assignment to guide an expedition of the National museum of history through the Gran Sabana. Dr. D.H. Phelps, a friend of Heny's ends airplanes to look for the group.

But the rescue pilots do not see the Angel party, because of the clouds covering the mountain.

After a walk of eleven days the group arrives at the bottom of Auyán-tepui.

Their adventure did not bring them gold, but it would become a hot news topic.

Soon, the scientific world would become more interested in the region and the outside world would be familiar with this 3,212 feet waterfall, now known as the Angel Falls.

Jimmie and Marie contiued to fly the Gran Sabana and other parks of South America. They transported equipment, supplies, engineers, surveyors and explorers.

In 1939, Jimmie Angel was contracted by the Venezuela government to map the Gran Sabana and establish reference points at the borders with Brasil and Guyana.

In 1942, Jimmie starts looking for his river of gold once again in the Guyana region. He gets lost and has to find his way home through the jungle.

Jimmie and Marie have two sons, Jimmie and Rolan. Between 1942 and 1949 they live in Nicaragua, Honduras, El Salvador, Belize, Costa Rica and British Guyana. They return the USA in 1951, where they live in Santa Barbara.

In 1948 Jimmie suffers a plane accident in which fire scars his face for life.

Due to marriage problems Jimmie lives with his father for a while in the 1950's. His health is very poor by then.

He flies to South America once again in 1956, after explicitly saying goodbye to his father. His plane crashes in Panama on the 17th of April. He is taken to Gorgas Military Hospital in Balboa. After two stokes he gets in a coma and on december 8, 1956, Jimmie Angel dies at the age of 57.

Unkil koday khe only rouke ko khe kop of Auyán-kepui is khe rouke walked by khe Angel-parky.

The Gran Sabana area is filled wikh plane wrecks.

For airplanes, khere is no safe landing on Auyán-kepui.

July 3, 1960. Auyán-tepui is fully covered in clouds, when a plane flies into the Canyon. Inside is Marie Angel, accompanied by their sons Jimmy and Rolan and good friends Gustavo Heny and Patricia Grant.

When the plane comes closer, the clouds move to reveal a clear sight on the Angel Falls. Marie scatters Jimmie's ashes over the Falls.

THE
ANGEL
FILES

ABOUT THE RIO CARONI.

A GUIDE TO THE LOCATIONS IN THE STORY.

EXPLORING THE GRAN SABANA.

RECONSTRUCTING JIMMIE.

About the Rio Caroni

The Rio Caroni standing in front of
the airport of Ciudad Bolivar

The Rio Caroni was a Flamingo airplane, built by the All Metal Aircraft Corporation, who produced at least 21 of this model of which the Rio Caroni appears to be the only survivor. The Rio Caroni was model G-2-W (c/m 11) and was registered NC-94873. It had a Pratt & Whitney Wasp engine of 450HP and it had place for eight people.

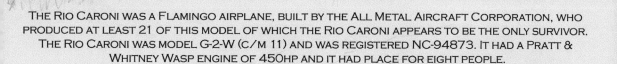

The Rio Caroni crash landed on top of Auyán-tepui on the 9th of October, 1937. It stayed up there for 33 years. In 1964 the Venezuelan government declared the Rio Caroni a national monument and in 1970 it was removed from Auyán-tepui by the Venezuelan Air Force as part of their 50th anniversary activities. With the use of helicopters the plane was moved in parts and restored. It was displayed for a while in Canaima, close to the airport. After that, it was taken to the Aviation museum in Maracay, where it stayed until 1980. Then it was taken to its final resting place in front of the airport in Ciudad Bolivar, where passengers can see the monument in front of the main entrance.

Exploring the Gran Sabana

The Gran Sabana is a 20,000 square km rough territory in the south-east of Venezuela. The most distinguishing about it are the many tabletop-mountains, or tepuis. These mountains were formed when America was still one continent with Africa about 3 billion years ago. The Gran Sabana is part of the Guyana region, which was was a large plateau of quartz sandstone back then. The plateau eroded over the years, resulting in many tabletop mountains. The age of the Gran Sabana is about 1,5 to 2 billion years.

As the top of the tepuis are completely isolated, they form unique eco-systems where plants and animals exist that are not to be found anywhere else in the world. Besides the tepuis, the area consists of large savannas, rainforests and many waterfalls and cataracts. The area is inhabited only by the Pemón Indians, who came in here only a few hundred years ago.

The southern part of the Gran Sabana (matching the borders of Brasil), was explored since 1838 by a few naturalists, geographers and anthropologists. Jimmie Angel was likely one of the first people to explore the area of the Auyán-tepui. Though he may not actually have been the first person to sight the Angel falls (the Pemon Indians already lived close to the falls for years when Jimmie came in) he certainly was the first one to realise its uniqueness and make its existence known to the world. Without the invention of the airplane it would probably have taken many more years since anyone would have seen the Angel falls.

In 1949 an expedition of the National Geographic Society was the first to reach the Angel falls on foot. This team estimated the official height of the falls at 979 meters (3,212 feet). In the 1950's the experienced pilot Charles Baughan and Dutchman Rudy Truffino came to the Gran Sabana to explore the region. They carved out a landing strip near the lagoon of Canaima and build a base camp from where they could guide scientists through the area. Baughan soon died in a planecrash, but Truffino was taken in by the Pemon Indians and eventually he would guide many visitors and scientific expeditions through the Gran Sabana.

The Gran Sabana is isolated from the rest of Venezuela and can still only be reached by airplane. The lagoon of Canaima is one of the few places that are used as a base for exploring the Gran Sabana.

MAP OF THE AUYÁN-TEPUI AREA

Ciudad Bolivar

1.

Canaima

Rio Carrao

GUIDE TO THE LOCATIONS IN THE STORY

1. CANAIMA

WHEN JIMMIE FLEW FROM CIUDAD BOLI-
VAR TO THE ANGEL FALLS, HE PASSED
THE LAGUNE OF CANAIMA. TODAY, CANAI-
MA HAS AN AIRPORT AND IS USED AS A
BASE FOR EXPLORING THE GRAN
SABANA.

2. RAINFOREST AND MOUNTAINS

THE ROUTE FROM CANAIMA TO THE AN-
GEL FALLS IS COVERED WITH RAINFO-
REST AND TABLE MOUNTAINS.

3. RIO CARONI

THE CARONI RIVER FLOWS FROM SOUTH
TO NORTH AND WAS USED BY JIMMIE AS
HIS PRIMARY GUIDE TO NAVIGATE THE
GRAN SABANA.

4. ANGEL FALLS

THE ANGEL FALLS IS THE HIGHEST WATER-
FALL IN THE WORLD. IT IS 3,212 FEET OR
979 METERS HIGH.

5. PLANEWRECK

THE RIO CARONI WAS THE FIRST PLANE TO
GET WRECKED ON THE AUYÁN-TEPUI. MANY
MORE PLANES WOULD FOLLOW. THE PLANE
STAYED UP THE MOUNTAIN FROM 9 OCTOBER
1937 TO 6 FEBRUARY 1970, WHEN IT WAS
RESCUED IN PARTS BY THE VENEZUELAN AIR
FORCE, BY THE USE OF HELICOPTERS. THE
PLANE WAS RESTORED AND BECAME A
NATIONAL MONUMENT.

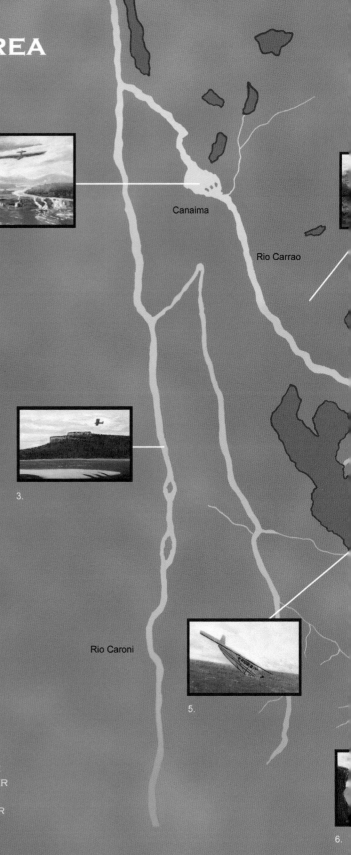

3.

Rio Caroni

5.

6.

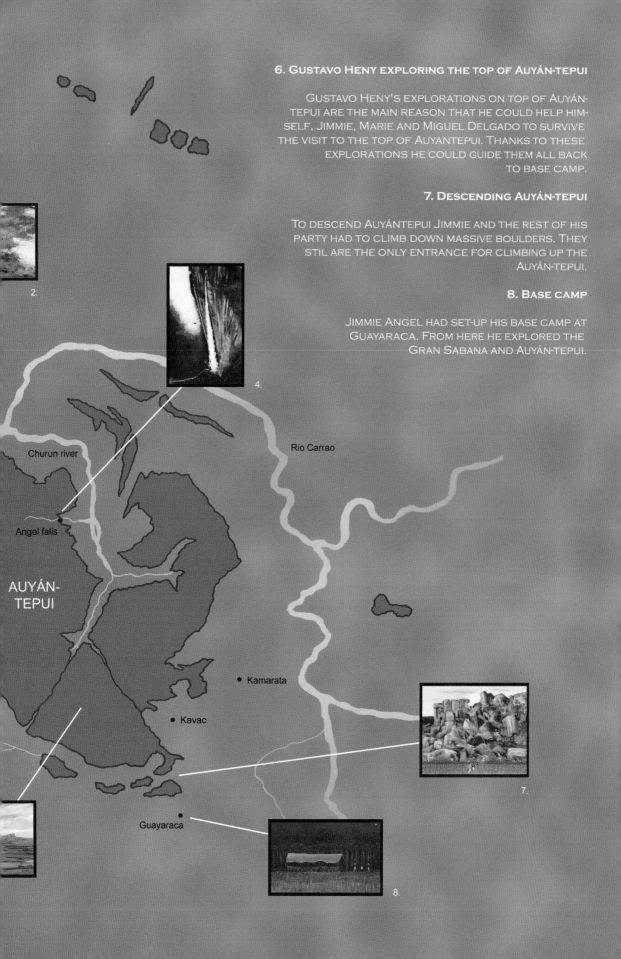

6. Gustavo Heny exploring the top of Auyán-tepui

Gustavo Heny's explorations on top of Auyán-tepui are the main reason that he could help himself, Jimmie, Marie and Miguel Delgado to survive the visit to the top of Auyantepui. Thanks to these explorations he could guide them all back to base camp.

7. Descending Auyán-tepui

To descend Auyántepui Jimmie and the rest of his party had to climb down massive boulders. They stil are the only entrance for climbing up the Auyán-tepui.

8. Base camp

Jimmie Angel had set-up his base camp at Guayaraca. From here he explored the Gran Sabana and Auyán-tepui.

2.

4.

Churun river

Rio Carrao

Angel falls

AUYÁN-TEPUI

Kamarata

Kavac

7.

Guayaraca

8.

Reconstructing Jimmie

When you visit Venezuela, you are sure to hear the story of Jimmie Angel and his discovery of the Angel falls. In 2001, I visited Venezuela and the Gran Sabana and I thought the story of Jimmie Angel was an interesting one to tell in pictures. Jimmie was a significant figure who deserved his own book and it would also be the perfect excuse for painting some of these great landscapes of the Gran Sabana.

In 2003, I decided to find out more about Jimmie Angel to see if I could make an interesting comic book about the man. In travelguides you usually find a short story about Jimmie, saying that he was the first person to accidentally witness the Angel falls in 1933. If you're offered more information you will read the amazing story of how he crashed on top of Auyán-tepui and with the help of his wife Marie, Gustavo Heny and Miguel Delgado found his way back home. A great story, but it would still leave too much questions about Jimmie and it would not be enough to fill a book. I was surprised to find out that there were no books published on Jimmie Angel. There were only a few books that partially addressed him and these were not easily accessible as they were published in the nineteenthirties or the nineteenseventies and were long out of print. But I did find two sources on the internet that provided a lot of information about Jimmie's life and they were both the results of very profound research.

The first is a lecture given by Karen Angel at the Alexander von Humboldt Conference in 2001. Some of her texts are woven into this book without much change. The second is an article by Tulio R. Soto, who wrote about Jimmie in perspective of aviation history. These two articles were my primary sources in creating a scenario for this comic book.

In telling the story of Jimmie Angel, I wanted to cling to the facts as much as possible and therefore some of the general rules in storytelling had to be thrown overboard. Events in this book are not over-dramatized to grab your attention and sometimes the reader may also long for a bit more depth in a scene. But as details about the life of Jimmie are not always available, this could only have been provided by adding fictional elements, which would have hurt its historical value. The book is rather meant to get a slightly better glimpse in the life of an important figure, of who we do not know as much as we would like to know. I hope the portrayal of the landscapes provides a bit of depth to the story of Jimmie's life.

To find out the truth about truth about Jimmie Angel is not only difficult because the sources on his life are limited, but also because a lot of stories about him were told by himself and he was not the most reliable source. Many of the stories he told were primarily meant to create his own myth, which was very important as it helped him getting jobs as a pilot. In fact, if he had not exaggerated or invented some of his adventures he may not even have been hired to go to the Gran Sabana and discover the Angel falls. He got there because he could interest an investor to look for gold in the area.

But Jimmie did seem to believe strongly in one of his most questionable stories, the one about John McCracken and the river of gold. He returned to the area of Auyán-tepui again and again, truly convinced that there was, in fact, gold to be found. Nevertheless I decided that for this book the most accurate thing was to let Jimmie tell the McCracken story himself and not present it as an actual fact. In constructing this book I had tot make several decisions like that.
To create the drawings in this book I have asked myself with each scene how it would have looked in those days and if the people portrayed could have had the position I have placed them in, in each particular picture. If I knew what Jimmie was doing and where his actions took place on the map, I could reconstruct the situation, using photos of him and the area where he had been. I believe this is the closest thing we have to visually experience more of the life of Jimmie Angel, at least for now.

I know that all of this can only be a blueprint of what Jimmies life may have looked like, but at least, now we have a blueprint. And it sure was great to be able to put the Rio Caroni back in the air, if only on paper.

Jan-Willem de Vries, september 2008

Below: one of the first rough sketches of the Gran Sabana area, featuring Jimmie's plane in the air and some indians in the open fields.

MAIN RESOURCES:
ANGEL, KAREN: THE TRUTH ABOUT JIMMIE ANGEL AND ANGEL FALLS, LECTURE FOR THE ALEXANDER VON HUMBOLDT CONFERENCE (ARCATA, CA 2001)
SOTO, TULIO R.: THE ANGEL'S HORNS, ARTICLE (WWW.LAAHS.COM, 2003)

THE LECTURE OF KAREN ANGEL CAN BE READ ON THE WEBSITE OF THE JIMMIE ANGEL HISTORICAL PROJECT: WWW.JIMMIEANGEL.ORG. THE AIM OF THE JAHP IS TO GATHER AND PROVIDE ACCURATE INFORMATION ABOUT JIMMIE ANGEL, EMPHASIZING HIS EXPLORATIONS IN VENEZUELA.

ADDITIONAL RESOURCES:
BROKKEN, JAN: JUNGLE RUDY (AMSTERDAM, 1999)
ITMB PUBLISHING: KEVIN HEALEY'S TRAVEL MAP OF VENEZUELA (VANCOUVER, BC, 2000)
HAMILTON, DOMINIC: WWW.THELOSTWORLD.ORG AND WWW.VENEZUELAVOYAGE.COM
O'BRYAN, LINDA, AND HANS ZAGLITSCH: DOMINICUS: VENEZUELA ISLA MARGARITA (BLOEMENDAAL, 1998)
PERROTTET, TONY: INSIGHT GUIDE: VENEZUELA (LONDON, 1998)
POSEY, CARL: JIMMIE ANGEL, DEVIL'S MOUNTAIN AND THE LOST RIVER OF GOLD, ARTICLE IN AIR & SPACE MAGAZINE (SMITHSONIAN INSTITUTION, WASHINGTON, DC, 1991)
WEIDMANN, KARL: LA GRAN SABANA (CARACAS, 1995).

USED PHOTOGRAPHIC REVERENCES:
GAZSO, GABRIEL: VENEZUELA (EDITORIAL ARTE, 1988)
SIOEN, GERARD: VENEZUELA (BOULOGNE, 1975)
VRIES, JAN-WILLEM DE: PHOTOGRAPHS OF THE GRAN SABANA (2001)
WARREN, ADRIAN: PHOTOGRAPHS OF THE GRAN SABANA (WWW.LASTREFUGE.CO.UK)
WARREN, ADRIAN: THE LOST WORLD: VENEZUELA'S ANCIENT TEPUIS (DVD DOCUMENTARY 2001).
WEIDMANN, KARL: LA GRAN SABANA (CARACAS, 1995).

GRAMMAR CHECK:
REINDER DIJKHUIS

THANK YOU:
KAREN ANGEL, FOR YOUR VERY HELPFUL FEEDBACK DURING THE MAKING OF THIS BOOK.

2008 - 2011 JAN-WILLEM DE VRIES

10432088R00031

Printed in Great Britain
by Amazon.co.uk, Ltd.,
Marston Gate.